Analogies
Grades 2-3
by Linda Ward Beech

SCHOLASTIC
PROFESSIONAL BOOKS

New York · Toronto · London · Auckland · Sydney
Mexico City · New Delhi · Hong Kong · Buenos Aires

Cover design by Andrew Jenkins and Kelli Thompson
Cover illustration by Kate Flannigan
Interior design by Glenn Davis
Interior illustrations by Maxie Chambliss

ISBN 0-439-27172-X

Contents

To the Teacher

Why Teach Analogies?

Analogies explore word—and therefore concept—relationships. Implicit in making analogies are numerous critical thinking skills. It is for these reasons that analogies appear on so many standardized tests.

Teaching analogies offers important and concrete benefits to students. Working with analogies

❖ expands students' vocabulary.

❖ enables students to look at words in new ways.

❖ helps students understand relationships between words and ideas.

❖ reinforces students' ability to make comparisons.

❖ increases reading comprehension.

❖ develops reasoning skills.

❖ prepares students for standardized tests.

Using the Book

The reproducible pages in this book provide step-by-step instruction in introducing and practicing five kinds of analogies. Students review the thinking skills needed for understanding each kind of analogy and become familiar with the formats in which the analogies appear. The THINK! component at the bottom of each page directs students to explain and explore their reasoning.

As you introduce each type of analogy or format, you'll want to model how to do it by thinking aloud. See the sample Think Alouds for each section.

Teacher Tip

Working in pairs or small groups gives students the opportunity to try out and explain their thinking as they work on analogies.

Examining Similarities (pages 8–13)

Analogies require that students recognize similarities in order to categorize words and ideas. Pages 8–10 provide practice in different kinds of grouping activities. Pages 11–13 require students to focus on the similarities between pairs of things.

Part/Whole Relationships (pages 14–19)

Page 14 Before students begin to recognize part/whole relationships, they need to understand what these are. This page provides an introduction to the concept. After students complete the page, have them review what the whole and the part is for each item.

Page 15 This page contains picture analogies. Begin by telling students that an analogy question gives two words (or pictures) that are related in some way. To complete the analogy, students must find two other words that are related in the same way.

Read the tip. Explain that the first pair of pictures is linked by this symbol [:]. The symbol [::] appears between the first and second pair of pictures. For each item, have students repeat the sentence: A (slice) is a part of an (apple), and a (leg) is a part of a (chicken).

Think Aloud

A handle is part of an umbrella. A zipper is part of what? A shoe? No, a shoe does not have a zipper. A sock? No, a sock does not have a zipper. A jacket? Yes, a jacket has a zipper. A handle is part of an umbrella, and a zipper is part of a jacket.

Page 16 This page reinforces the use of the part/whole sentence.

Page 17 Read the tip. Tell students that analogies are sometimes stated using the words *is to* and *as*. This page calls for students to explain their thinking about part/whole relationships.

Page 18 This page provides practice using analogies with the "is to" format.

Page 19 Read the tip. Review the symbol [:] and explain that it stands for the words *is to*. Review the symbol [::] and explain that it stands for the word *as*. The relationship between the first pair of words, *pitcher* and *team*, is part/whole, so the relationship between the second pair must be the same.

Teacher Tip

Remind students as often as necessary to read all the choices for an analogy before selecting an answer.

User/Object (pages 20–26)

Page 20 Before students begin to recognize user/object (or object/user) relationships, they need to understand what these are. This page provides an introduction to the concept.

Page 21 This page contains picture analogies. Begin by reviewing that an analogy question gives two words (or pictures) that are related in some way. To complete the analogy, students must find two other pictures that are related in the same way.

Think Aloud

A doctor uses a stethoscope. An ice skater uses what? A pair of ice skates? Yes, an ice skater uses a pair of skates. That might be the answer, but I'll read the other choices to be sure. A flower? No, an ice skater doesn't use a flower. A pair of scissors? No, an ice skater doesn't use a pair of scissors. I think a pair of ice skates is the answer. A doctor uses a stethoscope, and an ice skater uses a pair of skates.

Page 22 This page reinforces the use of the user/object sentence.

Page 23 Read the tip. Tell students that analogies are sometimes stated using the words *is to* and *as*. This page calls for students to explain their thinking about user/object relationships.

Page 24 This page provides practice using analogies with the "is to" format.

Page 25 Read the tip. Review the symbol [:] and remind students that it stands for the words *is to*. Review the symbol [::] and remind students that it stands for the word *as*. The relationship between the first pair of words, juggler and balls, is user/object, so the relationship between the second pair must be the same.

Teacher Tip

Let students know that the user/object analogy can also appear in reverse. Try practicing some of the user/object analogies provided in the form of object/user.

Page 26 This page reviews part/whole and user/object analogies. Be sure students understand that they are to first decide what kind of analogy it is (part/whole or user/object) and write the correct phrase. Students should then complete the analogy by filling in the circled letter by the correct answer.

Synonyms (pages 27–33)

Page 27 Before students begin to recognize synonym relationships, they need to understand what these are. This page provides practice with synonyms.

Page 28 This page contains picture analogies. Begin by reviewing that an analogy question gives two words (or a picture and a word) that are related in some way. To complete the analogy, students must find another picture and word that are related in the same way.

Think Aloud

A gift is the same as a present. A pair of pants is the same as what? A boy? No, a boy wears a pair of pants. Slacks? Yes, a pair of pants is sometimes called a pair of slacks. I'll read the last choice before I decide though. Shirt? No, a shirt is worn with pants, but I need a word that means the same as pants. So I think slacks is the answer. Gift is another word for present, and pants is another word for slacks.

Page 29   This page reinforces the synonym concept.

Page 30   Read the tip. Tell students that analogies are sometimes stated using the words *is to* and *as.* This page calls for students to explain their thinking about synonym relationships.

Page 31   This page provides practice using analogies with the "is to" format.

Page 32   Read the tip. Review the symbol [:] and remind students that it stands for the words *is to.* Review the symbol [::] with students and remind them that it stands for the word *as.* The relationship between the first pair of words, girl and gal, is synonym, so the relationship between the second pair must be the same.

Page 33   This page reviews part/whole, user/object, and synonym analogies. Be sure students understand that they are to first decide what kind of analogy it is and write it on the line. Students should then complete the analogy by filling in the circled letter by the correct answer.

Antonyms (pages 34–40)

Page 34   Before students begin to recognize antonym relationships, they need to understand what these are. This page provides practice with antonyms.

Teacher Tip

Suggest that students predict what the answer might be before they look at the answer choices, then look to see if their guess is there. Remind students that if the exact word isn't given as a choice, they should look for a synonym of their original guess.

Page 35   This page contains picture analogies. Begin by reviewing that an analogy question gives two words (or a picture and a word) that are related in some way. To complete the analogy, students must find another picture and word that are related in the same way.

Think Aloud

In is the opposite of out. Laugh is the opposite of what? Giggle? No, giggle is a synonym for laugh. I need the opposite of laugh. Cry? Yes, that seems right, but I will read the last choice to be sure. Smile? No, that is something you do when you laugh but it's not the opposite of laugh. In is the opposite of out, and laugh is the opposite of cry.

Page 36   This page reinforces the use of the opposite sentence.

Page 37   Read the tip. Remind students that analogies are sometimes stated using the words *is to* and *as.* This page calls for students to explain their thinking about antonym relationships.

Page 38 This page provides practice using analogies with the "is to" format.

Page 39 Read the tip. Review the symbol [:] and remind students that it stands for the words *is to*. Review the symbol [::] and remind students that it stands for the word *as*. The relationship between the first pair of words, do and don't, is two antonyms, so the relationship between the second pair must be the same.

Page 40 This page reviews part/whole, user/object, synonym, and antonym analogies. Be sure students first decide what kind of analogy each item is and write it on the line. Students should then fill in the circled letter of the correct answer to complete the analogy.

Name and Description (pages 41–47)

Page 41 Before students begin to recognize name and description relationships, they need to understand what these are. This page provides practice with nouns and adjectives.

Page 42 This page contains picture analogies. Begin by reviewing that an analogy question gives two words (or a picture and a word) that are related in some way. To complete the analogy, students must find another picture and word that are related in the same way.

Page 43 This page reinforces the use of the adjective and noun sentence.

Page 44 Read the tip. Remind students that analogies are sometimes stated using the words *is to* and *as*. This page calls for students to explain their thinking about descriptive relationships.

Page 45 This page provides practice using analogies with the "is to" format.

Page 46 Review the symbol [:] and remind students that it stands for the words *is to*. Review the symbol [::] and remind students that it stands for the word *as*. The relationship between the first pair of words, turtle and slow, is name and description, so the relationship between the second pair must be the same.

Page 47 This page reviews part/whole, user/object, synonym, antonym, and name/description analogies. Be sure students first identify the type of analogy and write it on the line. Students should then fill in the circled letter of the correct answer to complete the analogy.

Think Aloud

Glue is sticky. The sun is what? A moon? No, a moon is in the sky but it doesn't describe the sun. Bright? Yes, that sounds right but I'll read the last choice to be sure. Sky? No, the sun is in the sky but sky doesn't describe the sun. So, glue is sticky, and the sun is bright.

Examining Similarities

Grouping Things

Sort the things listed below into groups. Write each word from the list in the correct box.

doll

yellow

ball

apple

bread

green

game

red

pasta

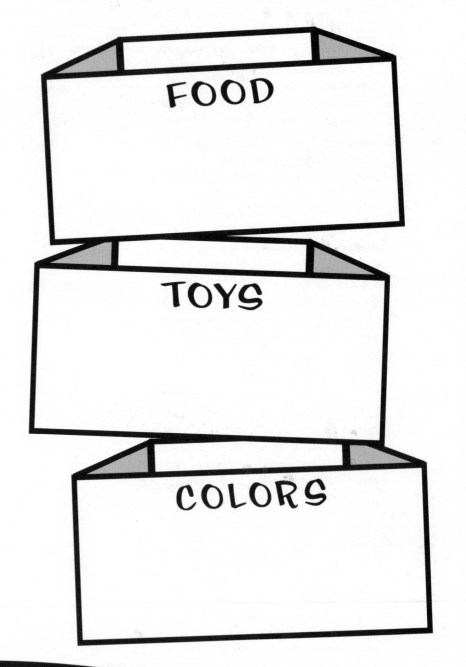

FOOD

TOYS

COLORS

THINK!
Look at the things in each group. Tell a partner how each thing fits into the group.

Examining Similarities

Kinds of Groups

Read each sentence. Write the correct word from the box to complete the sentence.

clothing	flower	dessert	tool
number	shape	animal	dish

1. A ⬭ is a kind of _____.

2. A 🌼 is a kind of _____.

3. A 🧥 is a kind of _____.

4. A 🧁 is a kind of _____.

5. A 🐔 is a kind of _____.

6. A △ is a kind of _____.

7. A 🔨 is a kind of _____.

8. A 6 is a kind of _____.

THINK!

Read the words in the box again. Think of another example for each group.

Examining Similarities

Name _____

Not in the Group

Read each list. Cross out the thing that does NOT belong.

1. seven
   short
   five
   one

2. arm
   neck
   toe
   bee

3. blue
   coat
   jeans
   dress

4. oak
   stone
   pine
   maple

5. hill
   pond
   lake
   river

6. bean
   carrot
   corn
   cup

7. house
   car
   bus
   truck

8. cry
   read
   sob
   weep

9. skip
   jump
   sleep
   hop

THINK!
Tell a partner why the word you crossed out does not belong in that group.

10

Examining Similarities

Finding Pairs

In each box a line connects two things that go together. Find two other things that go together in the same way. Draw a line to connect them.

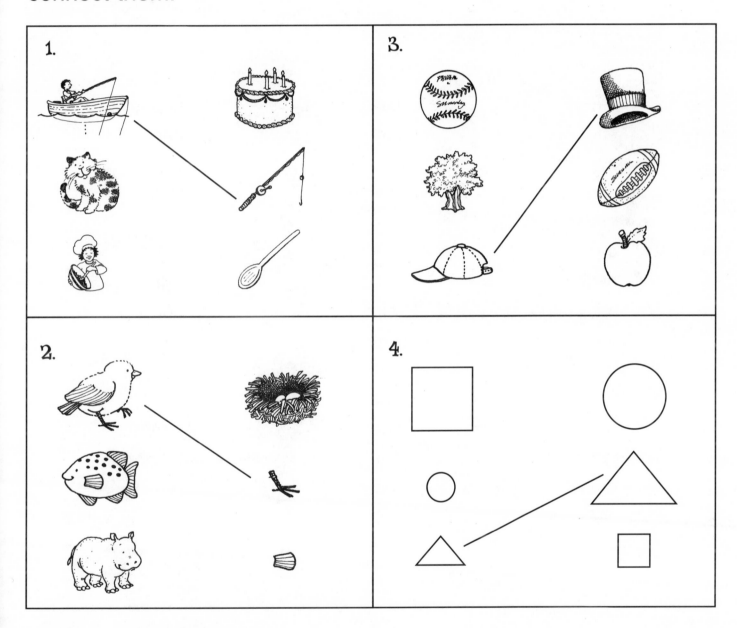

1.

2.

3.

4.

THINK!
Tell a partner how the pairs you matched in each box go together.

Examining Similarities

Finding More Pairs

In each box a line connects two things that go together. Find two other things that go together in the same way. Draw a line to connect them.

1. finger

    hat

    toe

2. purse

    milk

    letter

3. leaf

    sad

    moon

4. tiger

    shoe

    king

THINK!
Tell a partner how the pairs you matched in each box go together.

12

Examining Similarities

Picking Pictures

Think about how the first pair of pictures go together. Then look at the picture in the next box. Choose the picture that goes with it in the same way.

1. 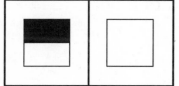 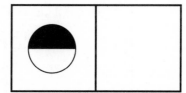 Ⓐ Ⓑ  Ⓒ

2.   Ⓐ Ⓑ  Ⓒ

3.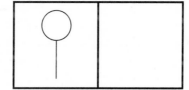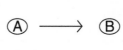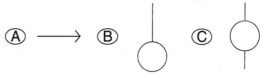

4.

5.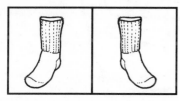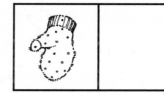

THINK!
Tell a partner why each picture you chose goes with the picture in the box.

Part/Whole Relationships

Name _____

Part of Something

Some things are parts of other things.
For example, a mouth is a part of a face.
Draw the missing part on each picture below.

1. A door is a part of a house.

3. A sail is a part of a boat.

2. A tail is a part of a dog.

4. A handle is a part of a cup.

THINK!
Choose one of the pictures. Name two more parts.

14

Part/Whole Relationships

●●

Parts and Pictures

Look at the first pair of pictures. Decide how they go together.
Choose the picture that completes the second pair in the same way.

   ::   :

Say to yourself: A slice is a part of an apple,
and a leg is a part of a chicken.

1. : :: : _____

   Ⓐ   Ⓑ   Ⓒ

2. :  :: : _____

   Ⓐ   Ⓑ    Ⓒ

3. : :: : _____

   Ⓐ   Ⓑ   Ⓒ

THINK!

Look at your hand. How many parts of
your hand can you name?

Part/Whole Relationships

Name _____

Pick a Part

Choose the correct word to complete each sentence.

1. A leg is a part of a table, and a seat is a part of a _____.
   Ⓐ rug   Ⓑ chair   Ⓒ bed

2. A string is a part of a harp, and a button is a part of a _____.
   Ⓐ shirt   Ⓑ snap   Ⓒ circle

3. A screen is a part of a TV, and a hand is a part of a _____.
   Ⓐ broom   Ⓑ clock   Ⓒ knob

4. A yolk is a part of an egg, and a pit is a part of a _____.
   Ⓐ peach   Ⓑ hen   Ⓒ word

5. A heel is a part of a foot, and an eye is a part of a _____.
   Ⓐ toe   Ⓑ nose   Ⓒ face

6. A stove is a part of a kitchen, and a couch is a part of a _____.
   Ⓐ den   Ⓑ sink   Ⓒ floor

7. A wing is a part of a bird, and a sleeve is a part of a _____.
   Ⓐ nest   Ⓑ sweater   Ⓒ pocket

8. A drawer is a part of a desk, and a pedal is a part of a _____.
   Ⓐ ladder   Ⓑ step   Ⓒ bike

THINK!
Name two things that each of these can be a part of: ear, eye, arm, leg, and neck.

Part/Whole Relationships   Name _____

○○

Telling Why

Read each sentence. Note the underlined words. Complete the second sentence to tell how the words in the second pair go together.

TIP | A <u>bird</u> is to a <u>flock</u> as a <u>wolf</u> is to a <u>pack</u>.
Say to yourself: A bird is a part of a flock,
and a wolf is a part of a pack.

1. A <u>hand</u> is to a <u>clock</u> as a <u>mouse</u> is to a <u>computer</u>.

   A hand is a part of a clock, and a _____ is a part of a _____.

2. A <u>pea</u> is to a <u>pod</u> as a <u>grape</u> is to a <u>bunch</u>.

   A pea is a part of a pod, and a _____ is a part of a _____.

3. A <u>letter</u> is to the <u>alphabet</u> as a <u>word</u> is to a <u>sentence</u>.

   A letter is a part of the alphabet, and a _____ is a part of a _____.

4. <u>Feathers</u> are to a <u>duck</u> as <u>fur</u> is to a <u>cat</u>.

   Feathers are part of a duck, and _____ is a part of a _____.

5. A <u>string</u> is to a <u>violin</u> as a <u>key</u> is to a <u>piano</u>.

   A string is a part of a violin, and a _____ is a part of a _____.

THINK!

Read your answers to a partner. Talk about what the answers all have in common.

○○○○○○○○

17

Part/Whole Relationships

A Part of What?

Look at the underlined words in each sentence. The first two words name a part and a whole. The third word names another part. Choose the word that names the second whole.

TIP

An <u>inch</u> is to a <u>foot</u> as a <u>minute</u> is to an <u>hour</u>.
Say to yourself: An inch is a part of a foot,
and a minute is a part of an hour.

1. A <u>day</u> is to a <u>week</u> as a <u>month</u> is to a _____.
   Ⓐ year   Ⓑ hour   Ⓒ second

2. A <u>tree</u> is to a <u>forest</u> as a <u>flower</u> is to a _____.
   Ⓐ garden   Ⓑ trunk   Ⓒ hill

3. A <u>grape</u> is to a <u>vine</u> as a <u>peach</u> is to a _____.
   Ⓐ weed   Ⓑ tree   Ⓒ pear

4. A <u>window</u> is to a <u>room</u> as a <u>porthole</u> is to a _____.
   Ⓐ ship   Ⓑ car   Ⓒ door

5. A <u>swing</u> is to a <u>playground</u> as a <u>barn</u> is to a _____.
   Ⓐ cow   Ⓑ slide   Ⓒ farm

6. A <u>paw</u> is to a <u>lion</u> as a <u>flipper</u> is to a _____.
   Ⓐ horse   Ⓑ hoof   Ⓒ seal

THINK!
Read your answers to a partner.
Tell why you chose them.

Part/Whole Relationships

Parts and Pairs

Read each word pair. Choose the word pair that goes together in the same way.

TIP	cap : pen :: lid : jar
	Say to yourself: A cap is part of a pen, and a lid is part of a jar.

1. pitcher : team :: _____
   - Ⓐ cook : meal
   - Ⓑ brick : stone
   - Ⓒ sailor : navy

2. cow : herd :: _____
   - Ⓐ fish : school
   - Ⓑ sweet : sour
   - Ⓒ jump : leap

3. elbow : arm :: _____
   - Ⓐ mitten : glove
   - Ⓑ tail : paw
   - Ⓒ knee : leg

4. fin : fish :: _____
   - Ⓐ puppy : dog
   - Ⓑ wing : bird
   - Ⓒ worm : snake

5. room : house :: _____
   - Ⓐ mug : cup
   - Ⓑ up : down
   - Ⓒ sink : kitchen

6. cover : book :: _____
   - Ⓐ story : tale
   - Ⓑ fork : cake
   - Ⓒ crust : bread

THINK!

Tell a partner how the word pairs you did not choose are related.

User/Object

Things We Use

People use different tools to do things. Read the list.
Draw a line from each player to the things for that sport.

1. baseball player

2. football player

3. tennis player

4. cyclist

5. hockey player

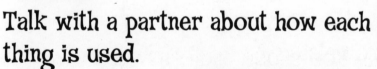

THINK!
Talk with a partner about how each
thing is used.

20

User/Object

Name _____

Who Uses What

Look at the first pair of pictures. Decide how they go together. Choose the picture that completes the second pair the same way.

 : ::  :

Say to yourself: A cook uses a frying pan, and a teacher uses chalk.

1. :  ::  : _____

Ⓐ  Ⓑ   Ⓒ

2.  : ::  : _____

Ⓐ  Ⓑ  Ⓒ

3.  :  :: : _____

Ⓐ   Ⓑ  Ⓒ

THINK!

Tell a partner why you chose each answer.

User/Object

Workers and Tools

Choose the best word to complete each sentence.

1. A <u>writer</u> uses a <u>computer</u>, and a <u>scientist</u> uses a _____.
   Ⓐ saw   Ⓑ microscope   Ⓒ drum

2. A <u>teacher</u> uses <u>chalk</u>, and a <u>rancher</u> uses a _____.
   Ⓐ rake   Ⓑ book   Ⓒ lasso

3. A <u>gardener</u> uses a <u>hoe</u>, and a <u>carpenter</u> uses a _____.
   Ⓐ hose   Ⓑ hammer   Ⓒ pen

4. A <u>dog walker</u> uses a <u>leash</u>, and a <u>golfer</u> uses a _____.
   Ⓐ club   Ⓑ bone   Ⓒ mop

5. A <u>boxer</u> uses <u>gloves</u>, and a <u>drummer</u> uses _____.
   Ⓐ coins   Ⓑ shorts   Ⓒ sticks

6. A <u>sweeper</u> uses a <u>broom</u>, and a <u>tailor</u> uses a _____.
   Ⓐ needle   Ⓑ soap   Ⓒ cane

7. A <u>letter carrier</u> uses a <u>bag</u>, and a <u>waiter</u> uses a _____.
   Ⓐ ball   Ⓑ tray   Ⓒ letter

8. A <u>batter</u> uses a <u>bat</u>, and a <u>dentist</u> uses a _____.
   Ⓐ crayon   Ⓑ drill   Ⓒ mitt

THINK!
Read your answers to a partner. Tell why you did not choose the other words.

User/Object

Making Connections

Read each sentence. Note the underlined words. Complete the second sentence to tell how the words in the first pair and the words in the second pair go together.

> **TIP** An <u>archer</u> is to an <u>arrow</u> as a <u>pitcher</u> is to a <u>ball</u>.
> Say to yourself: An archer shoots an arrow,
> and a pitcher throws a ball.

1. A <u>camper</u> is to a <u>tent</u> as a <u>teacher</u> is to a <u>desk</u>.
   A camper uses a tent, and a _____ uses a _____.

2. A <u>locksmith</u> is to a <u>key</u> as a <u>swimmer</u> is to <u>goggles</u>.
   A locksmith uses a key, and a _____ uses _____.

3. A <u>baker</u> is to <u>flour</u> as a <u>potter</u> is to <u>clay</u>.
   A baker uses flour, and a _____ uses _____.

4. A <u>skier</u> is to a <u>pole</u> as a <u>climber</u> is to a <u>rope</u>.
   A skier uses a pole , and a _____ uses a _____.

5. A <u>captain</u> is to a <u>boat</u> as a <u>driver</u> is to a <u>bus</u>.
   A captain sails a boat, and a _____ drives a _____.

THINK!

Read your answers to a partner. Talk about what the answers all have in common.

User/Object

Users and Uses

Look at the underlined words in each sentence. Complete each sentence with the word that names the tool the second person uses.

> **TIP** A <u>tour guide</u> is to a <u>map</u> as an <u>actor</u> is to a <u>script</u>.
> Say to yourself: A tour guide uses a map,
> and an actor uses a script.

1. A <u>baby</u> is to a <u>bib</u> as a <u>preacher</u> is to a _____.
   - Ⓐ crown
   - Ⓑ spacesuit
   - Ⓒ robe

2. A <u>traveler</u> is to a <u>suitcase</u> as a <u>hiker</u> is to a _____.
   - Ⓐ plow
   - Ⓑ canteen
   - Ⓒ hose

3. A <u>skier</u> is to a <u>ski</u> as a <u>skater</u> is to a _____.
   - Ⓐ bed
   - Ⓑ sled
   - Ⓒ skate

4. A <u>diner</u> is to a <u>spoon</u> as a <u>digger</u> is to a _____.
   - Ⓐ hook
   - Ⓑ shovel
   - Ⓒ hole

5. A <u>butcher</u> is to a <u>knife</u> as a <u>dressmaker</u> is to _____.
   - Ⓐ model
   - Ⓑ steak
   - Ⓒ scissors

6. A <u>weaver</u> is to a <u>loom</u> as a <u>painter</u> is to an _____.
   - Ⓐ easel
   - Ⓑ picture
   - Ⓒ artist

THINK!
Read your answers to a partner. Tell why you did not choose the other words.

User/Object

Finding Pairs

Read each word pair. Choose the word pair that goes together in the same way.

TIP

> juggler : balls :: gardener : seeds
> Say to yourself: A juggler uses balls,
> and a gardener uses seeds.

1. actress : make-up :: _____
   Ⓐ player : cards   Ⓑ wig : hair   Ⓒ costume : fancy

2. caller : telephone :: _____
   Ⓐ horse : ranch   Ⓑ speaker : listener   Ⓒ writer : paper

3. plumber : pipe :: _____
   Ⓐ batter : catcher   Ⓑ electrician : wire   Ⓒ doctor : nurse

4. farmer : tractor :: _____
   Ⓐ driver : rider   Ⓑ baker : cake   Ⓒ builder : bulldozer

5. reader : book :: _____
   Ⓐ tourist : map   Ⓑ clown : funny   Ⓒ seller : buyer

6. waitress : pad :: _____
   Ⓐ artist: canvas   Ⓑ steeple : church   Ⓒ drummer : band

THINK!
Tell a partner how the word pairs you did not choose are related.

Review

What Kind?

Read the first word pair. Write the phrase from the box that tells what kind of analogy it is. Then write the correct word to complete the second word pair.

Relationship:	Part/Whole	User/Object

1. knitter : needles :: actor : _____   Relationship _____
   - Ⓐ wool   Ⓑ cook   Ⓒ props

2. spout : teapot :: handle _____   Relationship _____
   - Ⓐ umbrella   Ⓑ hand   Ⓒ knob

3. lens : eye glasses :: pane : _____   Relationship _____
   - Ⓐ see   Ⓑ floor   Ⓒ window

4. diver : mask :: barber : _____   Relationship _____
   - Ⓐ chair   Ⓑ comb   Ⓒ swimmer

5. builder : brick :: printer : _____   Relationship _____
   - Ⓐ stone   Ⓑ singer   Ⓒ ink

6. card : deck :: bead : _____   Relationship _____
   - Ⓐ necklace   Ⓑ ruby   Ⓒ watch

THINK!

Tell a partner why it is important to know how the words in the first pair go together.

Synonyms

Almost the Same

Words that have the same or almost the same meaning are called synonyms.

Write a synonym for each word below.
Choose the words from the box.

weep	yell	shiny	small
skinny	big	speak	silly

1. thin : _____

2. large : _____

3. shout : _____

4. cry : _____

5. talk : _____

6. little : _____

7. funny : _____

8. bright : _____

THINK!

What other synonyms do you know for each word?

Synonyms

Look-Alikes

Look at the first picture and word. Decide how they go together. Then find a word to go with the second picture the same way.

 : auto :: : ship

TIP

Say to yourself: Car is another word for auto, and boat is another word for ship.

1. : present :: : _____

   Ⓐ boy   Ⓑ slacks   Ⓒ shirt

2. : sack :: **1** : _____

   Ⓐ single   Ⓑ two   Ⓒ kit

3. : chef :: : _____

   Ⓐ chair   Ⓑ sofa   Ⓒ living room

4. : carpet :: : _____

   Ⓐ treasure   Ⓑ bag   Ⓒ litter

THINK!
Tell a partner why you chose each answer.

Synonyms

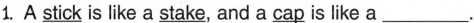

Same As

Choose the correct word to complete each sentence.

1. A <u>stick</u> is like a <u>stake</u>, and a <u>cap</u> is like a _____.
   Ⓐ sock   Ⓑ hat   Ⓒ twig

2. A <u>runner</u> is like a <u>racer</u>, and a <u>smile</u> is like a _____.
   Ⓐ frown   Ⓑ face   Ⓒ grin

3. A <u>crowd</u> is like a <u>mob</u>, and a <u>song</u> is like a _____.
   Ⓐ group   Ⓑ tune   Ⓒ flute

4. A <u>dinner</u> is like a <u>supper</u>, and a <u>pot</u> is like a _____.
   Ⓐ pan   Ⓑ cook   Ⓒ meal

5. <u>Fur</u> is like <u>fuzz</u>, and <u>wet</u> is like _____.
   Ⓐ messy   Ⓑ dry   Ⓒ damp

6. <u>Sad</u> is like <u>gloomy</u>, and <u>happy</u> is like _____.
   Ⓐ glad   Ⓑ mad   Ⓒ nice

7. <u>Misty</u> is like <u>foggy</u>, and <u>fast</u> is like _____.
   Ⓐ runner   Ⓑ quick   Ⓒ slow

8. <u>Look</u> is like <u>see</u>, and <u>sleep</u> is like _____.
   Ⓐ nap   Ⓑ wake   Ⓒ find

THINK!
Read your answers to a partner. Tell why you did not choose the other words.

Synonyms

Explaining Why

Read each sentence. Note the underlined words. Complete the second sentence to tell how the words in the first pair and the words in the second pair go together.

> **TIP** Stone is to rock as bug is to insect.
> Say to yourself: Stone is another word for rock,
> and bug is another word for insect.

1. Cap is to lid as spin is to turn.

   Cap is another word for lid, and _____ is another word for _____.

2. Shop is to store as stairs are to steps.

   Shop is another word for store, and _____ is another word for _____.

3. Boy is to lad as friend is to pal.

   Boy is another word for lad, and _____ is another word for _____.

4. Story is to tale as pail is to bucket.

   Story is another word for tale, and _____ is another word for _____.

5. Shiver is to shake as mad is to angry.

   Shiver is another word for shake, and _____ is another word for _____.

THINK!

Read your answers to a partner. Talk about what the answers all have in common.

Synonyms

Relating Word Pairs

Choose the correct word to complete each sentence.

 TIP A <u>sea</u> is to an <u>ocean</u> as a <u>guy</u> is to a <u>man</u>.
Say to yourself: Sea is a word for ocean,
and guy is a word for man.

1. A <u>gap</u> is to a <u>hole</u> as a <u>belt</u> is to a _____.
   Ⓐ sash   Ⓑ skirt   Ⓒ space

2. <u>Snip</u> is to <u>cut</u> as <u>pull</u> is to _____.
   Ⓐ tug   Ⓑ push   Ⓒ cross

3. <u>Ask</u> is to <u>beg</u> as <u>help</u> is to _____.
   Ⓐ need   Ⓑ aid   Ⓒ hurt

4. <u>Pick</u> is to <u>choose</u> as <u>chat</u> is to _____.
   Ⓐ talk   Ⓑ give   Ⓒ read

5. <u>Save</u> is to <u>keep</u> as <u>dislike</u> is to _____.
   Ⓐ give   Ⓑ hate   Ⓒ love

6. <u>Trap</u> is to <u>catch</u> as <u>toss</u> is to _____.
   Ⓐ throw   Ⓑ trip   Ⓒ lose

 THINK!
Read your answers to a partner.
Tell why you chose them.

Synonyms

Same Way Pairs

Read each word pair. Choose the pair that goes together in the same way.

TIP

girl : gal :: buddy : chum
Say to yourself: Girl is another word for gal,
and buddy is another word for chum.

1. dim : dull :: _____
   Ⓐ big : little   Ⓑ letter : word   Ⓒ brave : bold

2. almost : nearly :: _____
   Ⓐ beat : hit   Ⓑ writer : pen   Ⓒ old : young

3. bad : harmful :: _____
   Ⓐ weak : frail   Ⓑ empty : full   Ⓒ dog : tail

4. start : begin :: _____
   Ⓐ soft : hard   Ⓑ go : leave   Ⓒ bus : driver

5. eat : dine :: _____
   Ⓐ nap : doze   Ⓑ good : bad   Ⓒ ski : pole

6. make : form :: _____
   Ⓐ fast : slow   Ⓑ tub : sink   Ⓒ finish : end

7. grab : snatch :: _____
   Ⓐ jog : run   Ⓑ dig : cover   Ⓒ act : actor

8. firm : hard :: _____
   Ⓐ fly : plane   Ⓑ fair : right   Ⓒ sick : bed

THINK!
Tell a partner how the word pairs
you did not circle are related.

Review

Name the Pairs

Read the first word pair. Write the phrase from the box that tells how the words go together. Then choose the correct word to complete the second word pair.

Relationship:	Part/Whole	User/Object	Synonyms

1. tumble : fall :: howl _____   Relationship _____
   Ⓐ lion   Ⓑ trip   Ⓒ roar

2. shopper: money :: knitter : _____   Relationship _____
   Ⓐ sweater   Ⓑ yarn   Ⓒ sheep

3. battle : fight :: flag : _____   Relationship _____
   Ⓐ banner   Ⓑ country   Ⓒ parade

4. gate : fence :: door : _____   Relationship _____
   Ⓐ open   Ⓑ house   Ⓒ window

5. cap : bottle :: lid : _____   Relationship _____
   Ⓐ drink   Ⓑ off   Ⓒ jar

6. farmer : rake :: fisherman : _____   Relationship _____
   Ⓐ net   Ⓑ traveler   Ⓒ hoe

THINK!

Tell a partner why it is important to know how the words in the first pair go together.

Antonyms

Just the Opposite

A word that means the opposite of another word is called an antonym.

Write an antonym for each word below, using the words in the box.

sunrise	left	light	no
false	shut	soft	old

1. open : _____

2. sunset : _____

3. young : _____

4. dark : _____

5. right : _____

6. hard : _____

7. true : _____

8. yes : _____

THINK!
Make up some sentences using a pair of antonyms. Tell them to a partner.

Antonyms

Not Alike

Look at the first picture and word. Decide how they go together.
Then choose a word to go with the second picture the same way.

 TIP   STOP : go ::  : open

Say to yourself: Stop is the opposite of go,
and closed is the opposite of open.

1. : out :: He He! : _____

   Ⓐ giggle   Ⓑ cry   Ⓒ smile

2. : cold :: : _____

   Ⓐ warm   Ⓑ move   Ⓒ down

3. : sad :: : _____

   Ⓐ unhappy   Ⓑ hate   Ⓒ friend

4. : fix :: : _____

   Ⓐ dry   Ⓑ sew   Ⓒ mend

 THINK!
Tell a partner why you chose each answer.

35

Antonyms

The Opposite Of

Choose the correct word to complete each sentence.

1. <u>Rich</u> is the opposite of <u>poor</u>, and <u>weak</u> is the opposite of _____.
   Ⓐ strong   Ⓑ day   Ⓒ frail

2. <u>Give</u> is the opposite of <u>take</u>, and <u>ask</u> is the opposite of _____.
   Ⓐ get   Ⓑ answer   Ⓒ teacher

3. <u>Help</u> is the opposite of <u>harm</u>, and <u>work</u> is the opposite of _____.
   Ⓐ hurt   Ⓑ try   Ⓒ play

4. <u>Good</u> is the opposite of <u>bad</u>, and <u>rough</u> is the opposite of _____.
   Ⓐ smooth   Ⓑ bumpy   Ⓒ mean

5. <u>Over</u> is the opposite of <u>under</u>, and <u>near</u> is the opposite of _____.
   Ⓐ middle   Ⓑ far   Ⓒ here

6. <u>Warm</u> is the opposite of <u>cool</u>, and <u>safe</u> is the opposite of _____.
   Ⓐ afraid   Ⓑ cold   Ⓒ unsafe

7. <u>Cloudy</u> is the opposite of <u>sunny</u>, and <u>early</u> is the opposite of _____.
   Ⓐ late   Ⓑ day   Ⓒ timely

8. <u>Top</u> is the opposite of <u>bottom</u>, and <u>front</u> is the opposite of _____.
   Ⓐ whole   Ⓑ back   Ⓒ side

THINK!

Read your answers to a partner. Tell why you did not choose the other words.

Antonyms

○●○

Reasoning

Read each sentence. Note the underlined words. Complete the second sentence to tell how the words in the second pair go together.

TIP

<u>Follow</u> is to <u>lead</u> as <u>alone</u> is to <u>together</u>.
Say to yourself: Follow is the opposite of lead,
and alone is the opposite of together.

1. <u>Enter</u> is to <u>leave</u> as <u>push</u> is to <u>pull</u>.

   Enter is the opposite of leave, and _____ is the opposite of _____.

2. <u>Heavy</u> is to <u>light</u> as <u>plain</u> is to <u>fancy</u>.

   Heavy is the opposite of light, and _____ is the opposite of _____.

3. <u>Empty</u> is to <u>full</u> as <u>alike</u> is to <u>different</u>.

   Empty is the opposite of full, and _____ is the opposite of _____.

4. <u>Lost</u> is to <u>found</u> as <u>dim</u> is to <u>bright</u>.

   Lost is the opposite of found, and _____ is the opposite of _____.

5. <u>Live</u> is to <u>die</u> as <u>throw</u> is to <u>catch</u>.

   Live is the opposite of die, and _____ is the opposite of _____.

THINK!

Read your answers to a partner. Talk about
what the answers all have in common.

○●○●○●○●○

Antonyms

This Is to That

Choose the correct word to complete each sentence.

TIP | <u>Fresh</u> is to <u>stale</u> as <u>rise</u> is to <u>fall</u>.
Say to yourself: Fresh is the opposite of stale,
and rise is the opposite of fall.

1. <u>Real</u> is to <u>fake</u> as <u>hard</u> is to _____.
   Ⓐ work   Ⓑ easy   Ⓒ unreal

2. <u>Land</u> is to <u>sea</u> as <u>country</u> is to _____.
   Ⓐ city   Ⓑ farm   Ⓒ air

3. <u>Winter</u> is to <u>summer</u> as <u>fall</u> is to _____.
   Ⓐ year   Ⓑ season   Ⓒ spring

4. <u>Freeze</u> is to <u>melt</u> as <u>hide</u> is to _____.
   Ⓐ show   Ⓑ cover   Ⓒ dig

5. <u>Hello</u> is to <u>good-bye</u> as <u>sleep</u> is to _____.
   Ⓐ greet   Ⓑ doze   Ⓒ wake

6. <u>Above</u> is to <u>below</u> as <u>left</u> is to _____.
   Ⓐ right   Ⓑ center   Ⓒ top

THINK!
Read your answers to a partner.
Tell why you chose them.

Antonyms

Opposite Pairs

Read each word pair. Choose the word pair that goes together in the same way.

TIP	do : don't :: will : won't
	Say to yourself: Do is the opposite of don't, and will is the opposite of won't.

1. begin : end :: _____
   - Ⓐ stop : finish
   - Ⓑ listen : tell
   - Ⓒ curve : circle

2. smile : frown :: _____
   - Ⓐ stamp : tiptoe
   - Ⓑ look : gaze
   - Ⓒ book : read

3. win : lose :: _____
   - Ⓐ jog : run
   - Ⓑ card : deck
   - Ⓒ all : none

4. sick : well :: _____
   - Ⓐ narrow : thin
   - Ⓑ quilt : bed
   - Ⓒ big : little

5. day : night :: _____
   - Ⓐ north : south
   - Ⓑ dime : dollar
   - Ⓒ knock : tap

6. first : last :: _____
   - Ⓐ yell : shout
   - Ⓑ before : after
   - Ⓒ chew : eat

THINK!

Tell a partner how the word pairs you did not circle are related.

Name _____

Kinds of Pairs

Read the first word pair. Write the phrase from the box that tells how the words go together. Then choose the correct word to complete the second word pair.

Relationship:	Part/Whole	User/Object
	Synonyms	Antonyms

1. rower : oar :: welder : _____   Relationship _____
   Ⓐ sail   Ⓑ fire   Ⓒ torch

2. steal : rob :: whirl : _____   Relationship _____
   Ⓐ dancer   Ⓑ take   Ⓒ twirl

3. hub : wheel :: tooth : _____   Relationship _____
   Ⓐ tire   Ⓑ comb   Ⓒ fang

4. high : low :: sweet : _____   Relationship _____
   Ⓐ sour   Ⓑ candy   Ⓒ good

5. foot : yard :: leaf : _____   Relationship _____
   Ⓐ branch   Ⓑ inch   Ⓒ green

6. plus : minus :: more : _____   Relationship _____
   Ⓐ add   Ⓑ less   Ⓒ most

THINK!
Tell a partner why it is important to know how the words in the first pair go together.

Name and Description

What It's Like

Write each word from the list under the word that best describes it.

orange

lettuce

grass

knife

ball

marble

pencil

beans

pin

GREEN

SHARP

ROUND

THINK!
Make a list of other words that tell about each thing on the list.

Name and Description

Describing Things

Look at the first picture and word. Decide how they go together.
Then choose a word to go with the second picture the same way.

 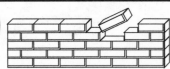 : brick :: 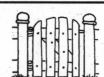 : wood

Say to yourself: The wall is brick, and the gate is wood.

1. : sticky ::  : _____ .

   Ⓐ moon   Ⓑ bright   Ⓒ sky

2. 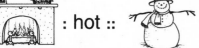 : hot :: 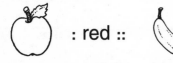 : _____ .

   Ⓐ cold   Ⓑ burning   Ⓒ thin

3. : red ::  : _____ .

   Ⓐ square   Ⓑ yellow   Ⓒ pink

4. : wool ::  : _____ .

   Ⓐ foot   Ⓑ sole   Ⓒ leather

5. : sweet :: : _____ .

   Ⓐ salty   Ⓑ sour   Ⓒ chew

THINK!
Tell a partner why you chose each answer.

Name and Description

How It Is

Choose the correct word to complete each sentence.

1. An ant is black, and a grasshopper is _____.
   Ⓐ blue   Ⓑ fuzzy   Ⓒ green

2. A shirt is cotton, and a jar is _____.
   Ⓐ glass   Ⓑ silk   Ⓒ jam

3. A hill is rolling, and a river is _____.
   Ⓐ winding   Ⓑ rainy   Ⓒ steep

4. A daisy is white, and a rose is _____.
   Ⓐ green   Ⓑ dirty   Ⓒ red

5. A ring is round, and a box is _____.
   Ⓐ wool   Ⓑ square   Ⓒ happy

6. An elephant is large, and a mouse is _____.
   Ⓐ small   Ⓑ huge   Ⓒ yellow

7. A puddle is muddy, and a pool is _____.
   Ⓐ sad   Ⓑ clear   Ⓒ shy

8. A hammer is hard, and a pillow is _____.
   Ⓐ sleepy   Ⓑ sharp   Ⓒ soft

THINK!
Read your answers to a partner. Tell why you did not choose the other words.

Name and Description

●○

Linking Ideas

Read each sentence. Note the underlined words.
Complete the second sentence to tell how the words in the
second pair go together.

> **TIP** <u>Coal</u> is to <u>black</u> as <u>salt</u> is to <u>white</u>.
> Say to yourself: Coal is black, and salt is white.

1. <u>Tent</u> is to <u>canvas</u> as <u>belt</u> is to <u>leather</u>.
   A tent is made of canvas, and a _____ is made of _____.

2. <u>Ribbon</u> is to <u>velvet</u> as <u>helmet</u> is to <u>plastic</u>.
   A ribbon is made of velvet, and a _____ is made of _____.

3. <u>Honey</u> is to <u>sticky</u> as <u>chips</u> are to <u>crunchy</u>.
   Honey is sticky, and _____ are _____.

4. <u>Fox</u> is to <u>sly</u> as <u>rabbit</u> is to <u>fast</u>.
   A fox is sly, and a _____ is _____.

5. <u>Beach</u> is to <u>sandy</u> as <u>cliff</u> is to <u>rocky</u>.
   A beach is sandy, and a _____ is _____.

THINK!
Read your answers to a partner. Talk about
what the answers all have in common.

Name and Description

Words That Describe

Look at the underlined words in each sentence. The first word names something, and the second word tells about it. Complete each sentence with a word that tells about the third underlined word.

TIP

> Tail is to curly as mane is to bushy.
> Say to yourself: A tail is curly, and a mane is bushy.

1. Corn is to yellow as beets are to _____.
   Ⓐ green   Ⓑ snack   Ⓒ red

2. A globe is to round as a map is to _____.
   Ⓐ flat   Ⓑ messy   Ⓒ bumpy

3. A bear is to hungry as a monkey is to _____.
   Ⓐ ape   Ⓑ playful   Ⓒ helpful

4. A carrot is to orange as peas are to _____.
   Ⓐ garden   Ⓑ farmer   Ⓒ green

5. A bridge is to steel as a road is to _____.
   Ⓐ tar   Ⓑ grass   Ⓒ car

6. Bacon is to crisp as eggs are to _____.
   Ⓐ raw   Ⓑ lunch   Ⓒ scrambled

THINK!
Read your answers to a partner. Tell why you chose them.

Name and Description

Name _____

A Pair and a Pair

Read each word pair. Choose the word pair that goes together in the same way.

 TIP
zebra : striped :: leopard : spotted
Say to yourself: A zebra is striped,
and a leopard is spotted.

1. turtle : slow :: _____
   - Ⓐ shell : snail
   - Ⓑ frog : toad
   - Ⓒ rabbit : fast

2. day : light :: _____
   - Ⓐ noon : twelve
   - Ⓑ night : dark
   - Ⓒ morning : evening

3. pearl : white :: _____
   - Ⓐ ruby : red
   - Ⓑ rock : stone
   - Ⓒ pin : ring

4. storm : windy :: _____
   - Ⓐ snow : ski
   - Ⓑ tie : untie
   - Ⓒ cloud : fluffy

5. attic : dusty :: _____
   - Ⓐ basement : damp
   - Ⓑ broom : sweep
   - Ⓒ hot : cold

6. sky : blue :: _____
   - Ⓐ misty : foggy
   - Ⓑ grass : green
   - Ⓒ sea : boat

THINK!
Tell a partner how the word pairs you did not circle are related.

Review

Kinds of Analogies

Read the first word pair. Write the phrase from the box that tells how the words go together. Then choose the correct word to complete the second word pair.

| Relationship: | Part/Whole | User/Object | Synonyms |
| Antonyms | Name and Description |

1. stinger : bee :: claw : _____   Relationship _____
   Ⓐ nail   Ⓑ tiger   Ⓒ hive

2. can : tin :: bag : _____   Relationship _____
   Ⓐ paper   Ⓑ carry   Ⓒ wood

3. add : subtract :: long : _____   Relationship _____
   Ⓐ short   Ⓑ minus   Ⓒ tall

4. slip : slide :: glow : _____   Relationship _____
   Ⓐ dim   Ⓑ glimmer   Ⓒ candle

5. banker : check :: singer : _____   Relationship _____
   Ⓐ dancer   Ⓑ bank   Ⓒ songbook

6. cup : china :: spoon : _____   Relationship _____
   Ⓐ fork   Ⓑ eater   Ⓒ silver

THINK!
Tell a partner why it is important to know how the words in the first pair go together.

Answers

page 8 Food-apple, bread, pasta; Toys-doll, ball, game; Colors-yellow, green, red

page 9 1. dish 2. flower 3. clothing 4. dessert 5. animal 6. shape 7. tool 8. number

page 10 1. short 2. bee 3. blue 4. stone 5. hill 6. cup 7. house 8. read 9. sleep

page 11 1. chef to spoon 2. fish to fin 3. baseball to football 4. small circle to large circle

page 12 1. foot to toe 2. milk to glass 3. sad to happy 4. lion to tiger

page 13 1. B, 2. A, 3. B, 4. C, 5. C

page 14 1. house with door 2. dog with tail 3. sailboat with sail 4. cup with handle

page 15 1. C, 2. B, 3. C

page 16 1. B, 2. A, 3. B, 4. A. 5. C, 6. A, 7. B, 8. C

page 17 1. – 5. Students should note that in each analogy, the first item in the word pair is a part of the second item.

page 18 1. A, 2. A, 3. B, 4. A, 5. C, 6. C

page 19 1. C, 2. A, 3. C, 4. B, 5. C, 6. C

page 20 1. cap, baseball; 2. helmet, football; 3. racquet, tennis ball; 4. bike, helmet; 5. skate, hockey stick

page 21 1. A, 2. B, 3. C

page 22 1. B, 2. C, 3. B, 4. A, 5. C, 6. A, 7. B, 8. B

page 23 1. – 5. Students should note that in each analogy the second word is something that the person in the first word can use.

page 24 1. C, 2. B, 3. C, 4. B, 5. C, 6. A

page 25 1. A, 2. C, 3. B, 4. C, 5. A, 6. A

page 26 1. C User/Object 2. A Part/Whole 3. C Part/Whole 4. B User/Object 5. C User/Object 6. A Part/Whole

page 27 1. skinny 2. big 3. yell 4. weep 5. speak 6. small 7. silly 8. shiny

page 28 1. B, 2. A, 3. B 4. C

page 29 1. B, 2. C, 3. B, 4. A, 5. C, 6. A, 7. B, 8. A

page 30 1. – 5. Students should note that the word pairs are synonyms.

page 31 1. A, 2. A, 3. B, 4. A, 5. B, 6. A

page 32 1. C, 2. A, 3. A, 4. B, 5. A, 6. C, 7. A, 8. B

page 33 1. C Synonym 2. B User/Object 3. A Synonym 4. B Part/Whole 5. C Part/Whole 6. A User/Object

page 34 1. shut 2. sunrise 3. old 4. light 5. left 6. soft 7. false 8. no

page 35 1. B, 2. C, 3. B, 4. A

page 36 1. A, 2. B, 3. C, 4. A, 5. B, 6. C, 7. A, 8. B

page 37 1. – 5. Students should note that the word pairs are antonyms.

page 38 1. B, 2. A, 3. C, 4. A, 5. C, 6. A

page 39 1. B, 2. A, 3. C, 4. C, 5. A, 6. B

page 40 1. C User/Object 2. C Synonym 3. B Part/Whole 4. A Antonym 5. A Part/Whole 6. B Antonym

page 41 1. Green-lettuce, grass, beans; Sharp-knife, pencil, pin; Round-orange, ball, marble

page 42 1. B, 2. A, 3. B, 4. C, 5. A

page 43 1. C, 2. A, 3. A, 4. C, 5. B, 6. A, 7. B, 8. C

page 44 1. – 5. Students should note that in each analogy the first word names an item and the second word describes it in some way.

page 45 1. C, 2. A, 3. B, 4. C, 5. A, 6. C

page 46 1. C, 2. B, 3. A, 4. C, 5. A, 6. B

page 47 1. B Part/Whole 2. A Name and Description 3. A Antonym 4. B Synonym 5. C User/Object 6. C Name and Description